Original title:
Tropical Hues

Copyright © 2025 Creative Arts Management OÜ
All rights reserved.

Author: Olivia Sterling
ISBN HARDBACK: 978-1-80581-582-2
ISBN PAPERBACK: 978-1-80581-109-1
ISBN EBOOK: 978-1-80581-582-2

Mango Mists

Mangoes dance in summer air,
Their sneaky peels, a fruity dare.
Boys chase drops on sandy floors,
While giggles echo by the shores.

Sticky fingers, laughter loud,
Chasing dreams beneath the cloud.
Juicy bites and laughter mixed,
In the sun, we're all transfixed.

Radiant Shores

Flip-flops squeak on sun-kissed sand,
As sunburned noses make their stand.
Seagulls squawk a cheeky tune,
While kids declare that now's their boon.

Kites soar high amidst a breeze,
Chasing waves with utmost ease.
Sandcastles rise, then tumble down,
A royal mess, the sand king's crown.

A Symphony in Saffron

Lemons laugh in cups of cheer,
Dripping yellow, never fear.
Saffron threads in soups do swirl,
As laughter joins the spice dance whirl.

A parrot squawks a roaring joke,
While silly hats provoke a poke.
With every sip, the joy's increased,
Our taste buds cheer, the fun's released.

Turquoise Dreams

Ocean waves in playful splashes,
Swimmers dodge the foam that crashes.
Blue-tinted shades on sun-kissed skin,
Fashion choices, let the fun begin!

Cocktails swirl in colors bright,
Straws like snails, a funny sight.
Laughter bubbles, joy's the flow,
In this paradise, we let it glow!

Wildflower Reverie

A dandelion in a hat,
Dancing with a cheeky cat.
Butterflies in flip-flops roam,
Turning flowers into foam.

Bumblebees wear goofy ties,
Swapping honey, sharing pies.
Laughing clouds that tickle trees,
Forgetful winds that hiccup breeze.

Afterglow Awakenings

Sunsets paint the sky with glee,
While coconuts sip herbal tea.
Parrots spinning in a jig,
Giggling at a silly pig.

Tanned beach balls bounce around,
Making friends where joy is found.
Sandy toes and sunburned noses,
Laughter blooms like blooming roses.

Sapphire Horizons

Waves that wear a turquoise crown,
Seagulls wearing little frowns.
Flip-flops on a wild escape,
Crabs that seem to dance and shape.

Sailing boats that wobble free,
Pretend to be a honeybee.
Giggles mix with ocean's sighs,
As fish put on their best disguise.

Golden Sands

Footprints lead to ice cream trees,
Where squirrels ride on bumblebees.
Sunshine wearing funky shoes,
Skipping free, sharing news.

Kites that dive in silly arcs,
Chasing shadows, leaving marks.
Golden grains that wink and shine,
Beaches filled with laughs divine.

Dawn's Citrus Whisper

Sunrise spills like lemonade,
Bouncing beams in bright cascade.
Lemons giggle on the trees,
As oranges dance in the breeze.

Parrots squeak a morning tune,
Waking up the sleepy noon.
Mangoes playing peek-a-boo,
Color mixed with silly view.

Bananas wear their sunny hats,
Chasing after cheeky cats.
Every fruit is in the game,
Silly shouts, a juicy fame.

Breezy laughter fills the air,
Swaying palms with playful flair.
Nature's joke is here to stay,
In this bright and fruity play.

Lush Reverie

Pineapples in jaunty shades,
Wearing sunglasses in the glades.
Kiwis giggle, ripe and round,
Making silly faces 'round.

Coconuts with goofy grins,
Floating gently, cheeky wins.
Mango salsa on a plate,
Dancing salsa, it's first-rate.

Grapefruits cracking jokes so loud,
While the sun shines, feeling proud.
Berries burst with laughter bright,
Underneath the golden light.

Cherries point and laugh with glee,
Swinging from the tallest tree.
In this garden of delight,
Fun grows brighter, day and night.

The Palette of Paradise

Colors splash like paint on leaves,
Sunshine giggles, no one grieves.
Pinks and yellows twirl around,
In a crazy dance they're found.

Limes are teasing, rolling near,
Making funny faces, dear.
Blue skies chuckle, bright and bold,
As laughter's threaded through the gold.

Each hue has a tale to tell,
From the peachy shade to shell.
Cacti wearing vibrant dress,
In this land we laugh no less.

Nature paints a comic scene,
With each shade, a bright routine.
Life's a canvas, fun and bright,
Every corner, pure delight.

Cobalt Oasis

Beneath the cobalt sky so wide,
Goofy turtles take their ride.
Splashing water, laughter flies,
As the fish wear silly ties.

A hammock sways, a dance of bliss,
Bananas plotting playful tricks.
Laughter echoes through the sand,
Life's a joke, so very grand.

Watermelons make a scene,
Sipping juice, they're so serene.
In this fun and sandy land,
Every fruit takes comic stand.

Seashells whisper silly lines,
Sunset paints its playful signs.
In the oasis, joy is real,
Every moment's a fruity deal.

Aroha in Bloom

In a garden full of smiles,
Sunflowers dance in bright piles,
Bees buzz in silly flocks,
Tickling each other's socks.

Laughter spills from wrinkled leaves,
While butterflies tease and weave,
Lemonade rivers flow with cheer,
As frogs croak songs we barely hear.

Mellow Mist and Memory

In soft shades of jammy cream,
The clouds roll by like a sweet dream,
A cat in a hammock, making a fuss,
With a fish who's too tired to discuss.

Whispers float like sheer confetti,
While a parrot practices a funny duet,
Grandma's laugh floats on the breeze,
As squirrels juggle nuts in the trees.

Melodies of the Moonlit Shore

The moon hums a goofy tune,
As clams throw a dance party under the moon,
Sandcastles groan with every wave,
While crabs break out the funk they crave.

Starfish wearing sunglasses bright,
Play limbo with all their might,
Oceans wink and toss their sands,
As giggles echo from the lands.

Crystalline Dreams

In a world where ice cream flows,
Slippers chase boys in funny clothes,
Jellybean trees sway with glee,
While jellyfish bounce on a rubbery spree.

Rainbows drip from candy skies,
As marshmallow clouds float by,
With gummy bears that dance and spin,
In a dream where silliness begins.

Citrus Blossoms

In the orchard, fruits collide,
Lemon-fresh and sweetly fried.
Oranges giggle, lime makes jokes,
Bananas join, a dance of folks.

Bees are buzzing, hats askew,
Pollinating with a stew.
A mango slips, then starts to roll,
It pops right up, and takes its toll.

Scent of citrus fills the air,
Lemons laugh without a care.
Juicy jokes from every tree,
A zesty bunch, just wait and see.

All together, what a sight,
Citrus party, pure delight.
Peels are tossed, a grand parade,
In this orchard, fun won't fade.

The Dance of Daisies.

Daisies twirl in sunlight's glow,
With floppy hats, they steal the show.
Petal shoes, on feet so spry,
They leap and spin, oh my, oh my!

Laughing stems in breezy glee,
Tickled by the bumblebee.
Each yellow center with a grin,
"Join the fun, please come on in!"

Wiggly worms, they feel the beat,
Dancing 'round with much more heat.
A daisy chain, the dance floor wide,
In nature's ball, they take such pride.

As dusk descends, they close their eyes,
Awaiting dreams beneath the skies.
Tomorrow's joy will come anew,
With daisy dreams and laughter true.

Island Whispers

Coconuts giggle on the trees,
Swinging around with a gentle breeze.
Papayas gossip, ripe and bright,
Sharing secrets through the night.

Oh, how the waves begin to clap,
As parrots wear a feathered cap.
Tropical fish flash their bright scales,
While sea turtles spin silly tales.

Sandy shores, a playful race,
Starfish compete in a silly chase.
Mermaids laugh as they comb their hair,
With seashells scattered everywhere.

Hammocks sway with a jolly tune,
Under the watch of the sun and moon.
Island whispers echo in delight,
Creating joy from day to night.

Sunlit Serenade

A sunflower sings to the sun,
Tickling petals, oh what fun!
Under bright beams, they start to sway,
In the warmth of a joyful day.

Lemonade breezes, ice cube songs,
Sipping sweet while nothing's wrong.
Bees are buzzing, joining the choir,
With buzz and hum that won't expire.

Picnic ants hold a grand affair,
Each crumb counts, they don't share.
Underneath the shady trees,
Everyone's laughing with the breeze.

As twilight falls, the stars come out,
Fireflies dance, no room for doubt.
In this sunlit serenade, we find,
Joyful moments, love unconfined.

Citrus Sunkissed

Lemons laugh beneath the sun,
Oranges dance, the day is fun.
Grapefruits grin in vibrant shades,
Each sweet bite, a joy parade.

Limes roll like they own the place,
Splashing zest with every trace.
Citrus jokes in every squeeze,
Life's a party, if you please!

Mangoes wear their sun-kissed robes,
While guavas boast their fruity prose.
Tasting joy in every chunk,
Who needs a thrill, when you've got funk?

Papaya chuckles, ripe and bright,
Pineapples party, pure delight.
In this garden, smiles abound,
Fruity laughter all around.

Hummingbird Harmony

Buzzing wings in vibrant flight,
Sipping nectar day and night.
Wiggly tails and silly hops,
Tiny dancers, never stops.

With colors that could sway a tree,
They flirt and tease so playfully.
In the bloom they prance and twirl,
Nature's charms in every swirl.

Their beaks dip low, then zigzag high,
Making us laugh, oh me, oh my!
Twirling in a sunny glow,
Their tiny antics steal the show.

These feathered jesters, quick and spry,
Bring a giggle as they fly.
In a world of whimsy and cheer,
They make happiness appear!

Jewel-Toned Skies

The sunset blushes, turquoise dream,
Magenta clouds, a laughing theme.
Goldfish giggle in the air,
Painted skies beyond compare.

Violet whispers on the breeze,
Emerald giggles through the trees.
Sapphire shimmies, skirts so bright,
Dancing with the stars at night.

Crimson hearts on canvas spread,
Casting shadows, laughter's thread.
Every hue, a playful wink,
Nature's palette makes us think.

As indigo takes nighttime's cue,
Daydreams spark, the fun is anew.
In the art of fleeting skies,
Every glance is a sweet surprise.

Enveloping Warmth

The sun wraps me in golden glee,
Like an oversized cup of tea.
Sweaty brows and goofy grins,
Warmth that makes the laughter spin.

Beach balls bounce like crazy fools,
While flip-flops dance in sandy pools.
Coconuts chuckle in delight,
As waves give seaweed a good fight.

Sun hats tip, suggesting fun,
"Come and play!" they say, "Let's run!"
Seagulls squawk a silly song,
In this warmth, we all belong.

Even the sun seems to agree,
Tickling toes in jubilee.
With every moment, joy cascades,
In this warmth, life never fades.

Palm Frond Fantasies

Underneath the swaying fronds,
A monkey steals my beachy snacks.
He wears a tiny sun hat,
And laughs at my sunburned backs.

The coconuts hang like old jokes,
Swinging low on their swish ropes.
I tried to juggle but fell down,
Now they all share in my hopes.

Woven Canopies

The leaves above weave a tale,
Of laughter and kite-flying whales.
A parrot squawks like a loud fool,
Announcing who's the biggest tool.

Under the vines, we sip on drinks,
With straws that twist like our thinks.
A lizard joins our funny spree,
And toasts our joy, quite fancily.

Seafoam Symphony

Waves dance like they're on a diet,
Slapping toes that just can't quiet.
A crab moonwalks in beachside glee,
While gulls sing songs of the sea.

Splashing water, laughter spills,
As dolphins dance with joyous thrills.
They wink, they twirl, they tease my hat,
Making me wish I was a cat.

Exotic Echoes

In jungle depths where echoes trade,
I found a raccoon with a spade.
He's digging for a treasure chest,
That holds the island's funniest jest.

The toucans laugh with beak-tied glee,
As I try to act like a tree.
In this wild and funny retreat,
Nature's quirks make life so sweet.

Lemonade Twilight

In a glass, yellow shines bright,
Sipping slowly in the light.
A grin spills as sugar meets,
The fizziness of sunny treats.

Sunset spills mischievous glee,
Birds are dancing on the tree.
The air hums with laughter's breeze,
As I spill my drink with ease!

I wear a hat that's way too tall,
While chasing butterflies that crawl.
My lemonade's now on my shoe,
I guess I'll call it "soda stew."

Now my shirt is stained with zest,
But hey, this party's truly best!
I squirted some on a friend's nose,
We giggle as our joy just grows.

Sun-drenched Soliloquy

Under sun in shades of gold,
I tell my secrets, bold and old.
My ice cream's melting down my hand,
Its drips form castles in the sand.

Seagulls laugh as they swoop down,
And steal my fries without a frown.
I chase them with an epic shout,
But they just circle round, no doubt.

A seashell whispers tales of sea,
Of fish who giggle, wild and free.
The sun's a joker, shining wide,
As I try to slip on a tide.

A crab scuttles, my snack in sight,
I chase it; oh, what a silly fight!
With splashes, laughter, and a puff,
I think this day is just enough.

Verdant Vibrations

In foliage bright, I skip and hum,
Where fruit hangs low and we can drum.
Bouncing vines with jokes to share,
I trip on roots, it's quite the dare!

Chickens cluck with rhythm and sass,
As I name them all with class.
A goat with shades joins in the play,
We laugh until the end of day!

The breeze brings melodies to tease,
Tickling my nose with leaves and bees.
I dance, I prance, a sight to see,
While slapping at the ants on me!

The colors swirl in playful gleam,
As nature joins my silly dream.
With laughter ringing through the trees,
I embrace the chaos with such ease.

Aqua Tranquility

Floating in a giant pool,
I'm the catch and sometimes fool.
My floaty's shaped like a big whale,
And I pretend I'm on a trail.

My friends are splashing with delight,
While I'm half drowning, what a sight!
Rubber ducks singing tunes they know,
Are judging me, but put on a show.

Underwater, I find my crown,
Made of leaves and a frown upside down.
I wave my arms like I can fly,
While mermaids laugh from a nearby fry.

A wave takes me for one wild ride,
Here comes a splash—we glide, collide!
With giggles that echo near the shore,
This poolside life, I do adore!

Cascading Colors

Bright hues collide, a playful game,
Pineapples dance, they want some fame.
Yellow and pink, they twist and twirl,
Coconuts giggle, join in the whirl.

Palm trees sway, they cannot stop,
One fell asleep, went kerplunk with a pop.
The sun's like a jester, shining so bright,
Throwing shadows in colors, a silly delight.

Balloons floating high, on a breeze they soar,
Laughter erupts as they all hit the floor.
Gone are the drab and dull shades of gray,
In this wild wonderland, come out and play!

Splashing in puddles, let's start a parade,
With flip-flops clapping, a featherweight charade.
In this land of laughter, full of cheer,
Who knew colors could make such a ruckus here?

Journey to the Emerald Isle

On a boat that creaks, we sail along,
With seagulls screeching their silly song.
Emerald waves crash, causing a scene,
As we throw in snacks, fish eat like a queen.

A crab in a tux, how bizarre is that?
He waves his claws, wearing a top hat.
We giggle and snicker, can't believe our eyes,
Nature's own jesters, what a funny surprise!

Shells play a game of musical chairs,
Who gets the prize? The one that declares!
We dive for the treasures, with glee and a splash,
While a dolphin waves, in a graceful dash.

Each step on the sand is a skit and a dance,
With waves as our beat, we give joy a chance.
This island is quirky, a laugh-crammed space,
Where laughter and colors embrace every face!

Wavelengths of Wonder

In a rainbow cabana, we host our affair,
With piña coladas, laughter fills the air.
The sun wears shades, like a diva so grand,
While waves chase seagulls, as if things were planned.

Fish in bright outfits swim by with a grin,
A group of them juggles, they're ready to win.
The octopus giggles, gets tangled in sea,
Dressed as a pirate, he's dancing with glee.

Flip-flops are flopping, a natural beat,
As mermaids cheer, they can't hide their feet.
They dive with a splash, send wild waves our way,
While laughter erupts, fueling this play!

In this zone of colors, find joy at its height,
Silly antics abound, on this dazzling night.
No time for the mundane, it's laughter that brews,
In the land of the vivid, where joy always coos!

Glimmering Beachwalks

The shells whisper secrets, oh what a sight,
As flip-flops parade in the soft moonlight.
Jellybeans bounce from a towel, they roll,
A candy cache hidden in a beachside hole.

Sandcastles stand, like kings in a row,
With gummy bear flags, we're putting on a show.
A crab in a suit leads the royal march,
While giggling kids give him a spirited arch.

The sun dips low, turning sky to a laugh,
As we chase down waves in a splashing half.
Sunburned noses, with ice cream on hand,
We skip and we stumble through this merry land.

Here's to the fun, in colors that scheme,
With memories sprinkled like sparkles on cream.
From shores of whimsy, our joys interlock,
In this gleeful paradise, we keep the clock!

Breeze-Kissed Blossoms

The flowers dance, they wave and sway,
In a wind that giggles night and day.
They wear their colors, bright and bold,
Like a circus act, a sight to behold.

Buzzing bees join the comical show,
In ridiculous hats, they steal the glow.
Petals whisper secrets in cheeky tones,
While butterflies juggle, with silly groans.

Sunshine winks from behind the trees,
Throwing confetti like it's a breeze.
Each blossom grins, a cheerful sprite,
In this garden party, pure delight!

Ocean's Palette

Waves wear jackets of creamy foam,
As crabs stage a parade, far from home.
Seagulls squawk jokes as they fly by,
Making splashy puns in the bright sky.

Fish flaunt their fins with glitter and glee,
Playing hide and seek with a cheeky sea.
Beach balls bounce in rhythm, oh so grand,
As sunbathers build castles, not quite planned.

The sunset paints with a brush of fun,
Mixing orange, pink, and a dash of pun.
Sandy toes share laughter, a brotherhood,
Where every splash feels incredibly good!

Vibrant Shores

At vibrant shores where the laughter rings,
Dancers twirl, flaunting their colorful things.
Shells play music with a clinking sound,
As happy footprints gather all around.

Umbrellas sway like they're part of the beat,
While kite-flying birds strut on their feet.
Sun-kissed bodies in hats askew,
Share sunburn tales that are far from true.

A beach ball bounces, a comet in flight,
Chasing giggles under the warm light.
Here joy's contagious, it spreads like goo,
On shores where every wave's a joke too!

Sunset Melodies

The sun dips low, a grand finale,
As crickets tune up for their joyful rally.
Chirping with glee, they play a refrain,
Of life's funny moments, sunshine, and rain.

Palm trees sway, like they've lost their way,
Grooving to music from the bright bay.
Clouds wear scarves of cotton candy,
While the sky bursts forth in colors dandy.

Laughter echoes as the stars peek through,
Twinkling like jewels in the night's blue.
In this melody of chaos and cheer,
Life plays on, with nothing to fear!

Sunset Serenade

The sun slips down, in a silly dance,
It trips on clouds, in a bright expanse.
Palm trees giggle, swaying with glee,
As coconuts chuckle from high, just to see.

A parrot squawks jokes, with feathery flair,
While waves make splashes, like a tuneful pair.
The horizon blushes, in hues quite absurd,
As laughter erupts from the bright, chirpy bird.

Bikini-clad folks, with ice cream in hand,
Slip on flip-flops, then dive in the sand.
The sun, now a clown, wears shades with a grin,
As night starts to chuckle, let the fun begin!

In this wacky show, where joy takes the stage,
All worries are gone, lost in the page.
So raise up your drinks, with umbrellas so bright,
Let's toast to the sunset, what a splendid sight!

Emerald Waves

Surfboards bouncing, they leap like a frog,
Waves roll in laughing, as light as a cog.
Sandcastles rise, but then quickly fall,
Oh, how they wail, a hilarious call!

Beach balls are bouncing, like joyful mice,
Each one that rolls, makes the kids giggle twice.
Inflatable turtles do the conga line,
While a crab on the shore rocks out with a spine.

Seagulls swoop low, with a quizzical peek,
Snatching up snacks, leaving crumbs in the creek.
Fishes in schools form a splashy parade,
While shells crack up, in an ocean escapade.

Emerald frolics, where fun never sleeps,
Each wave's a giggle, in secrets it keeps.
So let's ride the rhythm of this comical sea,
Where laughter and joy reign so wild and free!

Vibrant Canopy

In forests alive, where colors collide,
The leaves throw a party, with critters inside.
Monkeys swing 'round, in a game of charades,
While squirrels look on, in their nutty crusades.

Bright flowers gossip, they twist and they sway,
Sharing the news in a cheerful display.
The parrots are jesters, with feathers so bright,
Each joke that they squawk brings pure delight.

Lizards in shades, lounging up high,
Wink down below, with a glance and a sigh.
The trees clap their branches, in rhythm and rhyme,
As the sun beams down, giving laughter some time.

With a jungle so vibrant, where fun is the key,
Every corner hums with joyful decree.
So join the parade, let each moment sing,
In this lively canopy, let happiness spring!

Coral Skies

Clouds fluff like cotton, in a playful dream,
While giggles of sunset start to redeem.
Jellyfish float by, with jelly-like grace,
Doing the waltz in an undersea space.

Starfish cheer loudly, in their pointy attire,
While crabs tap their claws, setting the fire.
The ocean's a stage, where each twist and turn,
Brings laughter and joy, oh, how we yearn!

With coral reefs chuckling, in colors ablaze,
And fishes that flash through the coral maze.
The tide is our friend, in a humorous sway,
As sea urchins giggle, in their prickly play.

Beneath coral skies, where humor's the norm,
Life bubbles and chuckles, a delicate storm.
So let's dive right in, where the fun is alive,
Amongst all the creatures, let laughter thrive!

Petals in Paradise

In a land where parrots play,
Bright colors dance and sway.
A pineapple wears shades of blue,
As monkeys sip their morning brew.

Giggling flowers on the breeze,
Tickle bees with such great ease.
Coconuts with goofy grins,
Invite us in for silly spins.

A lizard struts in fashion bold,
His tail a tale that must be told.
With flip-flops on, he claims the street,
While sunbeams play beneath his feet.

Clouds above are marshmallow fluff,
As laughter bounces, bright and tough.
In this realm where dreams collide,
We find the joy that cannot hide.

Fragrant Journeys

A piña colada on a cart,
Sips of sunshine, oh so smart.
Banana peels like little boats,
Sail on drinks while laughter floats.

Pineapple pizza? What a thrill!
Let's try it with a side of chill.
Mangoes giggle, wrapped in cheer,
As guavas whisper, "Come right here!"

Funky hats with flowers bright,
Wobble gifts in silly flight.
We chase a breeze that tickles skin,
While fluffy clouds dare us to spin.

So pack your bags, let's take a ride,
On trains of joy, let's coincide.
With every snack, a funny tale,
In fruity lands, we are the sale!

Quiet Lagoon Lullabies

Beneath the palms, a hammock swings,
Where frogs compose their silly sings.
Lily pads in line parade,
While smiling turtles serenade.

The fish in shades of every hue,
Play leapfrog games, oh what a view!
A crabs' conga line rocks the shore,
While seagulls caw with jokes galore.

Gentle waves with slippery dreams,
Sprinkle giggles in sunbeams.
Ripples dance like kids at play,
Turning twilight into day.

Fireflies twinkle, stars above,
Each flicker whispers tales of love.
In this lagoon where fun takes flight,
We laugh until the late, late night.

Sun-Drenched Moments

Sandcastles rise with silly frowns,
As kids wear crowns made from brown downs.
A crab declares a royal quest,
While the sun gives it its best.

Ice cream drips on noses bright,
Flavors dance in pure delight.
A parrot teaches us to squawk,
As we gather 'round and mock.

Sunglasses on a crocodile,
Winks and giggles in this isle.
Surfers ride the laughter waves,
With pumpkin hats and silly braves.

Coconut drinks with crazy straws,
Raise a toast to funny flaws.
In the warmth of laughter's glow,
We find the joy in every flow.

Silken Skies

Up above, the clouds do dance,
In pink and purple, they prance.
A parrot squawks a silly rhyme,
As sunbeams play, and oh, what a time.

The breeze carries laughter down below,
Where flip-flops clash in a toe-to-toe.
Sun hats wobble on heads so bright,
While beach balls bounce in pure delight.

Coconuts join in a merry song,
As palm trees shimmy all day long.
With frosty drinks that drip and spill,
A sippy straw's a wild windmill!

Here, the skies stretch wide and gleam,
In a world that's just a fun-filled dream.
Beneath this canvas, smiles abound,
Where silly moments are always found.

Homage to Hibiscus

Hibiscus blooms, oh what a sight,
Shouting colors, pure delight.
With petals wide like funny hats,
They wave at bees and chirpy chats.

Each flower seems to wink and grin,
While butterflies swirl, and spin, and spin.
In gardens bright, where gnomes might snooze,
The plants all giggle in vivid hues.

A flower parade, oh what a show,
As ants march by, and dance in tow.
They tease the blooms, look here, look there,
In this wacky world, there's joy to share.

So here's to petals, bright and bold,
In a land of laughter and stories told.
These blossoms wink, they're quite the muse,
For all our quirky, joyful views.

Velvet Vistas

Rolling hills in shades of fun,
Catch the rays of the laughing sun.
Every curve's a playful jest,
Like nature's quilt, it's at its best!

The trees, they lean like pals in a game,
With vines that twist, they know no shame.
A swing set hangs from branches high,
Where clouds drift by and tickle the sky.

Fields of color, a sight to see,
Where clumsy bunnies hop with glee.
And every breeze brings giggles near,
As whispers float, we have no fear.

Oh velvet vistas, bright and loud,
Chasing dreams among the cloud.
In every nook, a smile found,
Where whimsy reigns and joy abounds.

Whispering Waves

Waves that chuckle, splash, and play,
Tickling toes, they sway away.
With each retreat, they tease and sneak,
Leaving footprints that giggle and peek.

Surfboards glide, a wild ride,
As laughter echoes with the tide.
Seashells scatter, join the fun,
With whispers swapping, one by one.

A crab does a dance, quirky and neat,
While seagulls squawk, quite the treat.
The ocean waves make witty art,
In a comical show, they break apart.

By sandy shores, where dreams arise,
With salty air and sunny skies.
So here's to laughter, waves that rave,
In a world where joy is what we crave.

Gemstone Groves

In velvety shades of lime and teal,
The monkeys dance with squeaky wheels.
Coconuts roll and crash, oh dear!
A pineapple slips, we all pop a cheer!

Parrots squawk with grand delight,
While iguanas join in a silly fight.
Under mango trees, we laugh and sway,
Fruit salad cheers at the end of the day!

The ground is soft like marshmallow fluff,
While ants parade, that's more than enough.
Lizards play tag, oh what a scene!
Giggling leaves in shades of green!

Each sound is a jolly, bouncing tune,
As laughter dances under the moon.
In these gemstone shades, we find our groove,
Who knew fun in nature could really move?

Twilight Tranquility

Sunsets blaze like a funny joke,
As fish jump out and try to poke.
Silly shadows start to prance,
While crabs in tuxedos join the dance!

The stars appear in a glittery spree,
Kittens chase fireflies, oh so free.
Apples hang from banana trees,
With giggles carried by a slight breeze.

On grass that smells like peppermint bark,
A turtle decides it's time for a spark.
He twirls and swirls, it's quite the sight,
And everyone joins in, oh what a night!

With winks from the moon, it's cozy and bright,
The world's a playground, and everything's right.
As waves crash softly with a tickle and tease,
Even the night knows how to please!

Radiant Shores

Sandy imps play hopscotch in the tide,
While a crab wears shades, full of pride.
Beach balls bounce with giggly grace,
Seashells laugh, it's a joyous race!

Surfboards wobble, a hilarious scene,
As surfers wipe out, it's not routine.
With sea cucumbers in a conga line,
This shoreline party feels just divine!

Seagulls squawk their own silly song,
While turtles strut, they just can't go wrong.
Under a sun that's blushing bright,
We gather and giggle till late at night!

Sandcastles sprout in flamboyant hues,
Flip-flops as hats, we can't lose!
Every grain of sand tells a funny tale,
Together we bask as we ride the gale!

Sunlit Canopies

Beneath the leaves, where giggles thrive,
We find funky fruits that come alive.
Swinging vines play peek-a-boo,
A toucan grins in a sky so blue!

Squirrels wear capes, and the orchids sway,
In a contest of laughter, who'll take the day?
Hummingbirds dive with a sparkling twist,
In this silly jungle, nothing's amiss!

Ferns do the cha-cha, all in a row,
While frogs serenade the ants down below.
With laughter and sunlight, we frolic and spin,
In this canopy, we all gather and grin!

The trees stand tall, like giants in glee,
While nature's comedy is wild and free.
In this leafy realm, we find our song,
In the joyful sundrops where we all belong!

Wind-Carved Dreams

Breezes dance with a silly flair,
Palm trees giggle, swaying with care.
Flip-flops squeak on the sandy floor,
While seagulls squawk 'Come back for more!'

Bright kites soar with a playful grin,
A dog steals snacks; oh, where to begin?
Children chase the waves, oh what a sight,
Sunburned noses from morning till night.

Funny hats wobble on heads of cheer,
Ice cream drips; hold on, my dear!
Shady spots where stories unfold,
These jolly moments are worth more than gold.

With colorful drinks that clink and fizz,
Every sip brings a cheerful whiz.
We laugh at the sunburns, one by one,
In this land where serious days are all done.

Celestial Coasts

Sunsets giggle, colors so bright,
Sandcastles topple, oh what a sight!
Crabs in tuxedos scuttle about,
In this ocean party, there's never a doubt.

Surfboards waiting, ready to glide,
A wave crashes, and splashes with pride.
Sunscreen battles, who's lost the most?
Laughter erupts, we're all a bit toast!

Tanning oil's spilled; oh what a mess,
Friends slip and slide in a sun-kissed dress.
Seashells whisper the tales of the sea,
Some look like hats, just wait and see!

With breezy winds playing hide and seek,
Seagulls swoop down, they're quite the sneak.
Stars peek out, like eyes in the night,
In this fun-loving realm, laughter takes flight.

Symphony of the Sun

Drums of the waves play a lively beat,
While sunbathers twirl in sun-kissed heat.
Silly dances erupt on the shore,
Where flip-flop melodies strike up a score.

The coconuts grumble, sharing their juice,
Sipping with straws, we'll let loose!
Beach volleyball bounces with joyous might,
Team shouts and slips, oh what a sight!

Tanned folks parade in mismatched tones,
Don't mind the laughter that brightly drones.
Pineapple hats wobble, what a parade!
In this grand concert, no notes will fade.

Sunburns gather patterns, a laughing affair,
Who knew sunglasses could make such a pair?
As twilight whispers, the fun carries on,
This symphony lingers, from dusk until dawn.

Cascading Color

Rainbows tumble from the sky's delight,
While surfboards glide in colorful flight.
Hawaiian shirts with patterns so bright,
  Make all passersby chuckle in sight.

Margaritas flow in glasses with flair,
With funny umbrellas dancing in air.
Fruit hats wobble as we shuffle by,
The end of the rainbow a silly lie!

Beach balls zoom with a bouncy cheer,
Each toss brings giggles drawing near.
Sandy footprints writing tales bold,
Of stories shared, and laughter retold.

With skies painted vivid, a playful show,
Everything's brighter where laughter can flow.
As the sun dips low, the colors collide,
In this joyful chaos, we dance and abide.

Jungle Heartbeats

The parrot squawks a silly tune,
As monkeys dance beneath the moon.
A sloth hangs low, with lazy style,
While toucans grin and chat a while.

The frogs croak jokes with glee at night,
With flashlights made of firefly light.
A jaguar winks at passing ants,
While lizards bust their funny pants!

Coconuts fall with goofy thuds,
As everyone's stuck in sticky muds.
The breeze brings laughter, quite absurd,
In the heart of where the wild things stir.

In this lush land, the humor spins,
Nature's laughs as joy begins.
From vines above, a punchline flies,
In every shade, the fun's the prize!

Rhythms of the Rainforest

The rain drops play a bouncy beat,
As critters sway and move their feet.
With each patter, a giggle stirs,
As dance-offs start with tiny furs.

Beetles strut in shiny shells,
While crickets tell the silliest tales.
A slapping monkey shows his stuff,
With such wild moves, it's quite enough!

Lizards chase their tails in dreams,
While ants march in with funny themes.
A butterfly flutters with a grin,
As every creature lets fun begin.

With rhythms loud, this party's grand,
In a wondrous, whimsical land.
Laughter echoes, joy takes flight,
In the rainforest, pure delight!

Luminous Tides

The sun dips low with shades that play,
While crabs slide sideways, what a display!
A dolphin jumps with a splashy cheer,
Shouting to fish, 'Come join me here!'

Starfish laugh in the sandy glow,
As waves bring giggles, high and low.
With bright shells spinning in the breeze,
Each creature dons a smile with ease.

The beach turns wild with cheeky fun,
As children race from sun to sun.
Sandcastles rise, then meet their doom,
While gulls squawk jokes that fill the room.

The tide rolls in, a joyful friend,
With every wave, the laughs ascend.
Under the light, moments we'll find,
Of silly joys that tie us entwined!

Under Canopy Light

The branches sway and giggles soar,
As squirrels plot from tree to floor.
With acorns tossed as secret gifts,
They giggle at the way the wind lifts.

A chameleon sneaks with colors bright,
Trying to blend in, oh what a sight!
He trips and flips, in laughter sprawls,
As echoing joy through the jungle calls.

The sun peeks through the leafy shade,
Creating shadows, a funny parade.
With dancing vines and ticklish air,
Each moment is filled with life and care.

So come join the wild, let spirits play,
Where laughter blooms in bright array.
Under the gaze of flickering light,
The forest whispers: "Life's a delight!"

Azure Dreams

In a sea of soda pop, how we sway,
Bright blue like jelly, we frolic and play.
Our toes in the sand, we jump and we leap,
While seagulls steal fries, oh, not in our keep!

A splash of cold water, the sun on our backs,
Hats blown away, we mend the big cracks.
The waves toss us high, like butter on toast,
With laughter that echoes, we're each other's host.

Bright shirts worn inside out, oh what a sight,
Dancing like fools, under stars burning bright.
We sip on our smoothies, with laughter and cheer,
Azure dreams twirl, making worries disappear.

Coral Reflections

Coral reefs tickle when fish start to laugh,
A crab in a tux, takes a selfie with gaff!
The anemones wiggle, with grins ear to ear,
Sharing tales of the currents, oh dear, oh dear!

Flip-flops a-floppin', we trip on the sand,
Chasing crabs feverish, a wacky parade.
A flamingo in shades says, 'Hey, take a break!'
With sun on our faces, our joy is at stake.

Mirrors of water, show us a dance,
Where sea cucumbers join in the romance.
With bubbles and giggles, we play 'who's a fish?'
Life's coral reflections grant the silliest wish.

Lush Labyrinths

In jungles so green, we wander and slide,
Lost in the leaves, we giggle and glide.
Monkeys throw coconuts, a raucous affair,
As parrots cackle loudly, with vibrant flair!

We trip over ferns, get tangled in vines,
Waddle like penguins, pretending we're shrines.
A sloth gives us pointers, with wise, sleepy eyes,
As if to say, 'Friends, slow dance with the skies!'

With every twist and turn, there's laughter anew,
Finding secret paths, painted shades of blue.
In lush labyrinths we play hide and seek,
Fun's captive essence, so silly and sleek.

Mango Skies

Mangoes are flying, it's raining sweet treats,
Under the sky where the sunshine competes.
We slip on our shades, and dive for a catch,
As sticky hands giggle, each crumb a new match!

The sun sets like juice, all vibrant and bold,
We joke about flavors, the warm and the cold.
It's a fruit-filled fiesta, where laughter takes flight,
In the dance of the clouds, every moment's delight.

With cheer that's contagious, we whirl in a spin,
Chasing our dreams, like the night's playful grin.
Mango skies promise, with flavors so ripe,
We'll savor this joy, without any type!

Lagoon Lullaby

Beneath the palm, a turtle sings,
While parrots dance on tiny swings.
A crab in shades, oh so bright,
Tries to boogie, what a sight!

Fish in suits, all decked and fine,
Join the party, sip a brine.
They splash and giggle, oh what fun,
Who knew sea life could be a pun?

A dolphin juggles seaweed hats,
While seagulls fight for tasty brats.
In every wave, a chuckle hides,
In this lagoon, where joy abides.

Tropical Tapestry

Sunsets paint with laughter wraps,
While monkeys play in sunny naps.
Parrots squawk their jokes so loud,
Wearing leaves instead of shrouds.

Coconuts fall, a thunderous cheer,
Sipping milk, the squirrels draw near.
They master tricks with sheer delight,
Jumping jigs, oh what a sight!

The breeze carries giggles and grins,
While iguanas play stringed violins.
All in colors, nature's glee,
Weaving tales of whimsy, you see!

Amber Sands

On amber sands, the crabs parade,
With tiny sunglasses, they're ready made.
They crack some jokes about seashells,
And toss the blooms with ocean swells.

A sandcastle stands, tall and proud,
As kids rank it, shouting loud!
The tide waves, "Ready, set, go!"
Time to watch that castle flow!

Seashells giggle, as they glide,
While starfish dance, the waves abide.
In this silliness, joy expands,
Living large on amber sands!

Effervescent Orchids

Orchids sprout with laughter draped,
In color bursts, so wildly shaped.
They tickle bees who dance and buzz,
Sipping nectar in a fuzzy fuzz.

A butterfly with polka dots,
Wears flower crowns; he's got the plots!
He tells a joke about his flight,
And all the petals sway with delight.

Orchids giggle, bright and spry,
As bumblebees hum by and by.
In this garden of vibrant schemes,
Joy blooms wildly, bursting seams!

Colorful Solitude

In a hammock strung between two trees,
The birds chirp tunes, a gentle tease.
I sip my drink through a bright blue straw,
While a lizard sidesteps with a comedic flaw.

Coconuts fall, like unripe jokes,
As I chuckle at an army of quirky folks.
A crab walks sideways, a dance so absurd,
I can't help but laugh at his little word.

Bright petals wink like they know a prank,
While shadows play tag by the garden bank.
Sunshine giggles, it has a sweet laugh,
As I muse over my colorful path.

Even the breeze can't help but jest,
Tickling me softly, a feathered guest.
In this pastel world of vibrant fun,
I embrace the chuckles, each and every one.

Daydream Drift

On a cloud of cotton candy dreams,
I drift away where nothing's as it seems.
Palm trees dance, wearing silly hats,
While a toucan plays chess with a pack of rats.

The ocean waves wink, they must be sly,
Making flip-flops float, oh me, oh my!
A crab competes in a race with the wind,
Cheering for shells, as the chaos rescinds.

I spot a bear, sipping a mango shake,
Dressed in a poncho, for goodness' sake!
He winks and says, "This is the life!"
While a sunburnt dolphin swirls in delight.

Drifting on daydreams, I'll never land,
With goofy friends in this radiant strand.
Smile as bright as a marigold bloom,
In this merry mirage, I find my room.

Resplendent Respite

In a colorful cabana, the sun's all ablaze,
Sipping sweet juice, lost in a daze.
A parrot squawks, sharing gossip so loud,
While a sloth munches on a leaf, so proud.

Rainbows peek through like curious eyes,
As I chat with a crab, oh how time flies!
With beach balls bouncing, in a whimsical air,
Life here is silly, without a care.

The sand tickles toes, in an endless dance,
And each grain is a ticket to joy's happy prance.
I laugh with the sea, sharing my secrets,
While donkeys in sunglasses roll by with some regrets.

The sun dips low, a plush orange hue,
While night brings out stars with a giggly view.
Here in this haven, I frolic with glee,
Embracing this respite, forever carefree.

Elysian Vistas

In a meadow where the wild colors play,
Butterflies gossip in the light of day.
A goat with a scarf struts with such flair,
While daisies chuckle without a care.

Clouds wear costumes, splendidly vague,
And every breeze carries a merry plague.
The sun has a grin, it's up to some fun,
As I race with the shadows, oh what a run!

Fields of fruit form a hilarious feast,
As I jive with a parsnip that dances at least.
A chorus of crickets plays tambourines,
As frogs join in with their wobbly scenes.

With each vibrant hue, laughter takes flight,
In this canvas of dreams, everything feels right.
I sway with the colors, so wild and spry,
In these elysian vistas, where spirits fly high.

Embered Horizons

The sun spills laughter on the sand,
As crabs perform a goofy dance,
With each wave that gives a hand,
Seagulls squawk like they're in a trance.

Palm trees twist in silly shapes,
Trying to tickle the breezy air,
While coconuts wear funny capes,
A nutty crown they proudly wear.

Flip-flops fling with joyful cheer,
Chasing toes that run away,
Splashing water crystal-clear,
As dolphins giggle in the bay.

Sunsets blend with bright confetti,
As night falls with a playful grin,
The stars blink back, all shiny, ready,
For our next whimsical spin.

Enchanted Isles

On islands where the coconuts beam,
A parrot jokes with all the guests,
Sipping piña coladas with a dream,
While hammock swings host their feasts.

Tiny crabs in a marching band,
Play a tune that's quite absurd,
While underfoot, they leave the sand,
In hopes we dance along, assured.

Clouds play peek-a-boo up in the sky,
Tickling palm fronds from afar,
Caught in winds, they soar and fly,
Like silly kites with laughs ajar.

The sun dips low on a fruity shore,
Ice cream drips, a colorful mess,
Waves roll in with a cheeky roar,
As we giggle at our sweet excess.

Lush Evening

As dusk arrives, the fireflies play,
Winking in their sparkling attire,
While mosquitoes hum a clumsy sway,
We swat and laugh—it's a comic choir.

Banana boats bob with a cheer,
As we glide on laughter and sun,
Fruit salads splash like a rainbow sphere,
With each bite, the giggles run.

Fluffy clouds grab the light of day,
Dancing like they've lost their shoes,
While palm fronds sway, lead the way,
As nighttime whispers, "Don't refuse!"

We gather round as stars appear,
Telling tales where punchlines dwell,
With every chuckle, cheer, and cheer,
Our hearts swirl like a merry bell.

Kaleidoscope Reflections

Mirrored waters laugh with glee,
Reflecting all our silly ways,
A fish flips by, oh what a spree!
In this bright world, who needs malaise?

Rainbow drinks in fizzing spritz,
With flavors darting left and right,
Sipping joy, we share our quips,
As the sun bows low to say goodnight.

Lanterns float like giggling stars,
Casting shadows that dance and tease,
As we strum our guitars from afar,
Tickling hearts with breezy ease.

In every laugh, a memory grows,
In this kaleidoscope of fun,
With every splash, the sunset glows,
Wishing endlessly we'd never run.

Indigo Oasis

In a land where coconuts dance,
And flip-flops have the best chance,
Bananas wear sunglasses too,
Laughing at clouds that are quite blue.

Parrots gossip with the breeze,
While turtles hitch rides with ease,
The waves join in with a hearty cheer,
There's a beach ball rolling without fear.

A hammock sways with a lazy grin,
As crabs play soccer to begin,
With jellybeans spilled all around,
Candy-coated laughter is found.

Under the Sun's bright survey,
Each silly game comes out to play,
In this joyful, colorful spree,
Everyone's as free as can be!

Dappled Sunlight

In a garden where giggles bloom,
Sunflowers wear hats, finding room,
Bees tap dance to a busy beat,
While ants parade with tiny feet.

Underneath the laughing trees,
Squirrels throw nuts like confetti,
A puddle's a mirror of glee,
Reflecting silliness for all to see.

Frogs croak jokes that make us smile,
With a splash, they hop in style,
The butterfly ballet takes flight,
Floating in colors, pure delight.

Each ray of sunlight tickles the air,
As laughter blooms without a care,
In this patch of fun-soaked cheer,
Every moment's a giggling sphere!

Fern-Flecked Pathways

On a pathway decked with greens,
Where laughter's mixed with nature's scenes,
A kangaroo trips on a shoe,
While the lizards giggle and construe.

Mice in sunglasses strut with flair,
As dragonflies humorously stare,
Dancing shadows play hide and seek,
In a world where fun is the peak.

A sign says, 'Beware of the slips!'
As winter hats volunteer trips,
We slide in colors bright and loud,
Chasing after a fluffy cloud.

With every fern and every twist,
There's a chuckle that can't be missed,
As nature joins this playful spree,
In pathways rich with jubilee!

Echoing Tides

Where the sea meets the sandy shore,
Waves tell jokes and ask for more,
With a splash they giggle and tease,
Dancing shells laugh on the breeze.

Seagulls swoop with a caw and spin,
While crabs play tag with a cheeky grin,
The horizon, a canvas of light,
Painting stories both silly and bright.

Fish in schools play syncopated,
In a world where laughter's fated,
Echoes bounce from sand to sea,
It's a chorus of joyous decree.

With each tide that tumbles and rolls,
The ocean calls to dancing souls,
In this vibrant stretch of glee,
Life is a splash, wild and free!

Frangipani Melodies

In a garden fraught with scents,
Frangipanis play hide and seek,
Bees buzz loud with no pretense,
  While lizards gawk and peek.

Coconuts drop with a thud,
A pair of ducks chase their tails,
Sand grins wide; it's pure fun mud,
The sun laughs, and the heat exhales.

Mango cheeks and juice galore,
  Each squirt a joyful surprise,
Sunscreen's war on a new chore,
With sticky hands and sticky skies.

Oh, the fruit that tumbles down,
Comedic slips give way to glee,
  In this land without a frown,
Where we live like wild and free.

Wildflower Sunlit

Petals pop like jokes on air,
Beehives laugh with busy hums,
A butterfly caught unaware,
Falls straight into the flower drums.

Daisies dance in cheeky cheer,
While ants parade their tasty loot,
Caterpillars shed a tear,
As they can't wear shoes or boots.

Sunlit rays play peek-a-boo,
A shadow tickles with delight,
Laughter skips like morning dew,
In this place where joy ignites.

Bees hold court, silk scarves in tow,
Every flower dons a smile,
Nature's laughter in full flow,
Let's stay silly for a while.

Azure Embrace

The sky winks with shades of blue,
Where sea turtles surf the waves,
Seagulls clap, 'You're doing great!'
While crabs pretend they are braves.

Shells giggle at each spunky splash,
As mermaids crack up on the rocks,
Sun is bold, no need to dash,
Sipping coconut milk from clocks.

Waves sass back with foamy curls,
Their tickles bring a smile wide,
Starfish flash their twinkly pearls,
As they wave to the silly tide.

In this fold of sky and sea,
Joy ebbs like tides at break of day,
In every splash, we're wild and free,
In every laugh, we find our way.

Palm Shadows

Beneath palms dancing in delight,
Laughter swings from branch to sand,
Chasing shadows, oh what a sight,
As coconut dreams take a stand.

Sunset's hues are knock-knock jokes,
Bouncing light like a jovial song,
Sandcastles built by silly folks,
With moats that look a bit wrong.

Flip-flops fling as kids run wild,
Surfboards play in sun's embrace,
Each squeal sounds like a happy child,
In this magical, sun-kissed place.

And when night wraps the view tight,
Fireflies join the merry spree,
Palm shadows dance in the moonlight,
Joy echoes as we all just be.

www.ingramcontent.com/pod-product-compliance
Lightning Source LLC
Chambersburg PA
CBHW072122070526
44585CB00016B/1529